TO LIVE AND DIE IN SCOUDOUC

HERMÉNÉGILDE CHIASSON

TO LIVE AND DIE IN SCOUDOUC
translated by Jo-Anne Elder

icehouse poetry

First published in French as *Mourir à Scoudouc* in 1979 by Les Éditions d'Acadie.
This edition is based on a new edition published in 2016 by Les Éditions Perce-Neige.

Edited by Ross Leckie.
Cover image by Herménégilde Chiasson.
Cover and page design adapted by Julie Scriver from the orginal by Herménégilde Chiasson.
Photographs by Herménégilde Chiasson with the exception of: Louise Blanchard (p. 90); Denis Lanteigne (pp. 16, 25, 36); Carol Nadon (p. 91); Guy Parent (p. 88); Louise Soucy (pp. 72, 76, 85, 94).
Printed in Canada.
10 9 8 7 6 5 4 3 2 1

Library and Archives Canada Cataloguing in Publication

Chiasson, Herménégilde, 1946-
[Mourir à Scoudouc. English]
    To live and die in Scoudouc / Herménégilde Chiasson ; translated by Jo-Anne Elder.

Translation of: Mourir à Scoudouc.
Poems.
Issued in print and electronic formats.
ISBN 978-1-77310-035-7 (softcover).--ISBN 978-1-77310-036-4 (EPUB).--
ISBN 978-1-77310-037-1 (KINDLE)

I. Elder, Jo-Anne, translator II. Title. III. Title: Mourir à Scoudouc. English

PS8555.H465M613 2018   C841'.54   C2017-906118-6
                                                 C2017-906119-4

We acknowledge the financial support of the Government of Canada through the National Translation Program for Book Publishing, an initiative of the *Roadmap for Canada's Official Languages 2013-2018: Education, Immigration, Communities*, for our translation activities. We also acknowledge the generous support of the Government of Canada, the Canada Council for the Arts, and the Government of New Brunswick.

Goose Lane Editions
500 Beaverbrook Court, Suite 330
Fredericton, New Brunswick
CANADA E3B 5X4
www.gooselane.com

He began with the ink of his painstaking obsession, wondering if it would be worthy of a book.

He began to write with a belief in the enclosed mystery, the revelation of the words.

He began with the figment of a day when they would lock into the ultimate combination.

He began to write, to imagine he would say what others had meant to say or not known how to say.

He imagined himself the bearer of their secrets, the causes of their misery, the silence of their decline.

TO

TO

RIMBAUD FROM THE SOUNDINGS OF THE NIGHT

I tore the sheet of paper into the pieces of myself, becoming the confetti falling from that stranger, wilder pinnacle. And I saw myself as the white of stainless snow sliding through sky, striking the earth with the inexplicable clang of cutlery. I was looking for the night. I had forgotten the afternoons of my childhood. I heard the carnage of suns I had crushed in my fists like small oranges dripping their light, like the tongues of Pentecostal fire I no longer expected. I ate on myself. There was no salt or pepper, no soup or bread.

I tore the sheet of paper into the pieces of myself, becoming the confetti falling from the stranger, wilder pinnacle of snow, of the air; this moment like the sun through the leaves, like an autumn afternoon, like a cloud filled with water, like bread on the table, like the sun that tosses gold on the snow of my country and into the hair of children.

AS IF...

To the stronger
To more than before
To the much softer April breeze
To clouds that linger
To those who make snow
To those who make nothing
To those who make music
To my eyes that cannot stop opening
To my hair on strike against zeal
To the leaves held prisoner by their trees
To crucified paintings flattened against walls
To my feet suffocating in their boots
To your body pinned to the landscape
To your image
To the fade out fade in fade around and back and forth
To the bye-byes
To teletypes that breed banal poems and weep at night
To automobiles and their cargo of human flesh
To snowflakes yes!
To all the snowflakes one by one
To the snowflakes that fall as we would fall into
celestial sorrow and the purity of snow, the bed of snow
like a wide clearing of noodles
like a river of soup encased in aluminium
And I open my heart like a wooden star with its arms sawn off
And I say the gates of heaven will open too.

BETWEEN
THE SEASON...

BETWEEN THE SEASON OF MAD LOVE
AND THE SEASON OF RASPBERRIES

You left, opening cracks in the April ice that melted so quickly, without noticing the spring as it hastened to come that year with a mild March wind that pasted leaves back onto the trees.

And you left so quickly that part of me was exiled within you; you left by roads, through puddles of water, bogs, gaping wounds in the asphalt bleeding muddy water onto our white clothes.

And I wondered if I would end up crossing the pale grass of the burnt-over clearings and the fresh water of the spring thaws in this journey that I took without a return ticket to visit a garden of untroubled flowers.

There were cabbages growing nearby, and someone gave me a bouquet of lettuce. Dusk was falling, and cars plunged into the night with the clamour of refugees reaching the border.

I shut the garden gate. A bouquet of forget-me-nots had been placed on the table. I opened the door of the house once again and outside the raspberries had begun to ripen.

SO YOU WON'T FLY AWAY

You have the eyes of birds about to fly away.
I would like to write to you with new words so you will hear me say in
a new voice that I would like to learn once again to speak the language
of green-feathered birds, to tell you to stretch the borders of paradise, to
push with both hands against the clouds that shrink the sky, to carve out a
sun for every day, to talk to you as though you were the last word I would
speak; to take your heart in my hands to hold it in your body, to prevent
it from getting cold so that you won't fly away; to tell you with words as
warm as your body what we will call ourselves when there are no more
words between us and when you are my most beautiful bird circling
around a white sun over a white river; to create a spring for you like a wide
field of ripening strawberries, so that you can find a perch and build your
nest under the birches. And the clouds working loose from the sky will
make the rain fall from my eyes, because you have the eyes of birds about
to fly away.

ALL THE KING'S HORSES

All the king's horses have died together, my love.
All the horses have died in the wide blue river.
But at the bottom of my river, crushed beneath the cadavers, I arose and
stepped forward, carrying the harness of my dead horse.

All the king's horses have died together, my love, in the wide blue river. But
there was no longer a king to rule over the rivers. The kings had forgotten
that they were kings, they had forgotten they were alone, and that without
love they would die with the horses that had fallen asleep, never to waken
again. I believe it was yesterday.

All the king's horses have died and we have died, too. We slipped into
the water under the soft, cold pelts of black horses, splayed and gutted,
bleeding red into the blue of the river.

le 11 janvier 1773.

Ils t'ont arraché les yeux et ils n'ont
laissé dans ton visage en sang qu'une
langue à ne rien faire, des paysages
calcinés qui te traînaient sur les lèvres
et une grande rivière de sang qui a
marbré ton corps de rouge en roulant
par-dessus ton coeur, ralenti dans tes
poils avant de descendre lentement de
chaque côté de ton sexe en éclair de
douleur sur tes jambes, et se sont enroulées
les lignes malheureuses de ta rivière éclatée
qui montait autour de tes pieds et
~~coulaient~~ en rigoles entre tes chevilles en
passant par-dessus tes veines qui
blanchissaient à mesure qu'elles se vidaient.

Toi qui saignait des yeux, mon amour
Toi qui saignait des yeux
Et moi qui pleurait du coeur
Toi qui voulait t'en aller et moi qui
voulait redescendre en esquif par la
rivière rougeoyante où se miraient les
paysages pétrifiés en inventant des ampoules
dans mes mains de rameur et nos visions
réchauffées.
Sur le rivage j'essayais d'étouffer dans mes
oreilles la solitude des cornemuses et les
violons débauchés les manitous qui dansent
en brandissant leurs bâtons remplumés.

ta descente devenait audacieuse.
Je ne me fie plus à mes yeux.
Plus rien que la maison à la porte clouée
du dedans pour la fête dont nous serons
témoins par la fenêtre à la vitre éventrée

JANUARY 11, 1973

They plucked out your eyes and left on your bloody face only a tongue
that could not move, charred landscapes that lingered on your lips and a
wide river of blood that marbled your body with red flowing over your
heart, slackening as it passed through your pubic hair before dripping
slowly down your genitals, pain flashing through your legs, tangled in the
mournful current of the shattered river rising around your feet and circling
in ripples around your ankles as it travelled over veins blanching as they
emptied.

You, bleeding from the eyes, my love
You, bleeding from the eyes
And I, crying from the heart
You who wanted to leave and I who wanted to float on a skiff down a
flaming river reflecting petrified landscapes, inventing calluses on our
rowers' hands, visions warmed over. On the riverbank I tried to stifle
the solitude of bagpipes and the broken-down visions of eternal spirits
wielding their feathered sticks as they danced.

The descent became steeper.
I no longer trusted my eyes.
Nothing more than the house with the door nailed shut from inside for the feast we would witness through the glass of the fractured house.

We will no longer go into the woods
We will no longer go anywhere
We will write letters in April stamped with the thaw of our nerves in this land of exile, while we wonder if the rescuer who knocks at our door looks like the Sandman or Santa Claus.

We are without a passport in the halls of a hospital enlarged by the last melting snows that screams on night's dissection table. Nail-headed stars hold up the sky in the air over our heads.

We are blind tourists, mute orators, deaf poets, musicians with amputated fingers, and filling the space between us, large stains of silence nailed to the sky's assumption of clouds.

Nous n'irons plus au bois
Nous n'irons plus nulle part
Nous nous écrirons des lettres en avril
timbrées du dégel de nos sensations dans
le pays d'exil pendant que l'on vérifie
par la porte pour voir si le libérateur
ressemble au bonhomme sept heures ou
au Santa Claus.

Nous sommes sans passeport dans les
corridors d'un pays-hôpital agrandi par
les dernières neiges fondantes d'une nuit
qui râle sur la table de dissection et
d'étoiles en têtes de clous qui retiennent
le ciel en l'air sur nos têtes.

Nous sommes des touristes aveugles, des
orateurs muets, des poètes sourds; des
musiciens aux doigts coupés et pour
emplir l'espace entre nous, de grandes
taches de silence cloué au ciel parmi
les nuages assomptif.

Nous sommes la voix décolorée, décrépie
des vieux jours sirotants, alors que tu
dansais en collant ton visage contre
la pluie.

Nous sommes assez vieux, assez loin pour
voir le jour des rivières de sang se
jeter dans les fleuves de lumière audacieux

Nous les oiseaux de braise
Nous les cormorans en sang
Nous les goélands au bec coupé

avec des étoiles sur le cœur et la tête

We are tarnished voices, decrepit old drunks sipping while you dance with your face raised towards the rain.

We are old enough, far enough away, to remember when streams of blood flowed into the rivers of impudent light.

We are the birds of ashes
We are the cormorants of blood
We are the gulls of clipped beaks

Stars on our hearts and heads in saliva

LISTEN TO YOURSELF

Just a minute. Listen to yourself. Listen to your heart ticking in every corner of your tired body. Listen to the longing, the desire, sinking to the depths of your chest. You can no longer hear the intermittent noise of doors closing or the buzzer that makes the whole building shriek with pain. No one visits at three o'clock in the morning, not even when the building is empty.

Pink and yellow papers flapping on walls, trying to tear themselves off, allowing themselves a last tryst, twisting in the ribbons of cooling air, torqued with joy and desire as they tried to press up against the wall. The unwarranted pain of things pressed against each other. The end of the blue world.

Outside: stars, shards of light floating in the abyss. Outside: the last night. Outside: my last love. Outside I see through large holes cut out of the sky. Ropes hanging from the ceiling, stretching along the venetian blinds, without knowing their own sad, pedestrian existence. Ropes falling from the ceiling. Ropes flowing down from the ceiling. Lascivious ropes surrendering themselves to radiators on fire.

I look at myself in the window. I wear a blue shirt and I place my finger on my lips. My hair is parted on the left and my eyes are heavy with despair. I am almost happy.

I am happy because I am more together than I have been. I am becoming unstuck like the papers on the walls, like the chairs nonchalantly lounging on the floor, like the lights that are trying their best, like the desks that are waiting patiently, like the windows that open relentlessly. I am an immense book filled with so many stories, illustrated in colour. I feel the urge to bite into pieces of iron, to melt the walls of ice in my body, to stretch out my arms and stroke the tops of the trees, to run my hand along the length of the sky, to lift the soft clouds of water, to die, arms plunged into the earth down to its heart.

SLIDING

Upon an appeal by petition to the authority of eviscerated doves, with the authority of words grown weary, the birds of peace were writing on the blue paradise, letters filled with last year's snow. Trees were stretched out in the snow listening to the murmurs of the North Pole.

We went out at the end of the afternoon like letters on children's wooden blocks. Letters that we had not written to each other. Nor did the telephones ring to tell those who listened the implausible, tedious, and compulsive vulnerability of words that no one dares speak. Night raps at our window, but inside, I no longer listen.

It was a night to be read from one corner to the other, an invitation to dawdle, to turn against the earth's rotation, clouds strung in garlands, fringes of canopies making me forget the sun beating my heart and the doves falling headfirst around our bed, staining our sheets red.

CAKE OF ENNUI

We ate up the night's towering cake frosted with the sugar of ennui, nights of love in every layer. We raised our eyes to watch angels pushing dreams with magnetic wands across scenery, like admirals moving fleets.

We see only the bars of daylight carving the night of our prison walls, we who are the prisoners of the continents and who watch the advancing fleets enclose our dreams, while we eat up the vast blue cake of night, while stars tear at our throats, while the river of our dispossessed dreams is smothered by the silence of the rising sun.

We are dying and yet we have eaten up the night's towering cake frosted with the sugar of ennui, nights of love in every layer.

DO YOU UNDERSTAND…NOW?

The underside of the world
On the other side of the world
The world upside down
Have you seen the top of the world from above?
The top of a world as others see it
Paradise in someone else's corner of the world
Paradise where trees grow
like crazy people crashing through the sky
until they reach the sunlight at the water's edge on the other side
The other side
No, don't say that!
It's not the other side of a world of others
with paradise, a big eye looking, a cyclops in the sky
in the pools of film catching fire,
in the smoke of projectors
The upside is inside
Inside, it is like a cage lit with neon
and Christmas candles and flaming cathedrals illuminated by the
gratitude of the faithful.
You don't need to be on the other side
None of it is true.

We don't need to enter paradise
Nor do we have to say that we have the sun just to burn the days on calendars

Do you understand ... now?
No, you still don't understand!
If you understood
you would still want to
clasp hands and be
lifted up into paradise
like a column of water.
You are not the Messiah!
If the Messiah returned today,
He would be unemployed.

IN ACADIE...

The afternoons when the gusts were so strong before you started school, when the clouds took their time travelling from one edge of the sky to the other.
The days when the doors wouldn't close properly and someone opened them for you.

When it was sunny enough to colour the blades of grass yellow
When it was blue enough that the sea began to rise
When the autumn tide in its coupling drowned the sorrows of the earth
When my brother painted Évangéline shielding her eyes with her hand to look away from Acadie

A carved wound, a legend vibrating across uneven floorboards, the blue of a water-logged schooner out on the sea, its beauty, its white sails whipping.

In Acadie as in a religious order.
White Mass, wedding in white across the troubling forests, death on the run from sleep, flat on your back, arms crossed over rifles and snow-bound vengeance.

In Acadie as in a deportation.
Englishmen with pointed helmets, red coats, polished boots of domination, supremacy trampling our clover fields, standing at attention awaiting orders from Boston, fugitives clinging to the earth's crust or shifting from north to south, from people to nation, from a casual embrace to love.
Lament of birch leaves fuelling smokeless fires awaiting the day they will conquer the bite of the cold in our skulls.

En Acadie ...

Les après-midi de grands vents quand
tu n'allais pas à l'école, quand les
nuages mettaient du temps à se transporter
de bord en bord du ciel.
Les journées où les portes fermaient mal
et que on te les ouvrait

Quand il faisait assez soleil pour colorer les
brins d'herbe en jaune
Quand il a fait assez bleu pour que la
mer commence à monter
Quand la marée d'automne a noyé dans
sa copulation le chagrin de la terre.
Quand mon père peignait Evangéline
qui met sa main sur ses yeux pour
regarder au loin de l'Acadie

Creusée en blessure, légende en chaloupe à
travers les planches pliantes, la beauté bleue
en départ de goélette dégoulinante en mer
et battant voiles blanches,

En Acadie comme en religion.

Messe blanche, mariage en blanc à travers
les forêts inquiétantes, la mort en fuite
dans le sommeil sur le dos, les bras en
croix sur les fusils de la vengeance enneigée,

En Acadie comme en déportation.

Anglais au casque pointu, red coat bien
chaussé de la domination, en suprématie
dans nos champs de trèfle ; au garde à
vous en attendant les ordres de Boston,
fugitif attachés à l'écorce ou mutation
de nord en sud, de peuple en pays, de

THE TRUE STORY OF EVANGELINE ··· THE TRADGIC
MOMENT ··· THE SEPERATION OF EVANGELINE (EM-
MELINE) AND GABRIEL (LOUIS). THE SCATTERING
OF THE ACADIAN COLONEY.

In Acadie as in a lamentation.

Hunting for dreams, warehouse of illusions, mirror of doubts, writing through bouts of vomit to blacken the inarticulate pages and forget the hallucinatory cry of animals that with agony raise their heads from the current as they cross the river.

And I was once again beginning to find it unbearable to watch the flight of birds soaring through the afternoons of strong winds that peeled the leaves from the trees and projected them into the cleavage of the seasons.

ACADIE
MY ALL-TOO-
BEAUTIFUL
LOVE

EUGÉNIE MELANSON

Neither fresh-water necklaces
Nor the smoking censers that priests hold aloft at the Feast of Corpus
Christi
Nor Good Friday banners
Nor the yellow stars, the red, white and blue flags
Nor loves lost, nor loves permitted still,
All of these pale to your beauty, Eugénie Melanson
You whose photo has come down through the years
To beckon to me
One June afternoon, when the sky was too blue and the sun was sinking
too low over a country that was no longer mine

You were the loveliest, all the same
Of course others have told you this, but I see your stark eyes, turned
inward, so as not to notice the years passing over forgotten beauty
You were the loveliest, all the same
When you dressed up as Évangéline, with the tacky Gabriels strutting on
parade, the memorable dates of our inglorious past, swallowed in dreams
long gone, the old poems you had never read
You were the loveliest, all the same
When one Sunday afternoon a photographer passing through town
caught your eighteen-year-old loveliness and set down through the slow
painstaking process, the imperfect remnants of your astonishing candour,
the slow and almost faint desire to remain here, now and forever, peering
out at the sun fading in the sky one last time, yes, simply one last time

You were the loveliest, all the same
Because one Sunday afternoon this photograph came into existence and
because one June afternoon you looked at me and made me pause
You were peering over the top of your black gown, your face pressed
against the glass
You were watching, though looking deep into your body, your eyes could
no longer see

You were watching, Eugénie Melanson, I know you were

The blue display cases, the religious objects, the lace-lined cradles, the axes hanging in the work shed, the ploughs no longer turning the fields, the Victorian furnishings of people who were wealthier than you, you remember, the gas lanterns that flickered near the doorway when, on windswept autumn evenings, your suitors came to lead you to the porch, you watched the birch logs in the fireplaces, you who had always dreamed of them, you remember, you watched the sleighs that surged across the snow on Sunday afternoons when it was time for vespers at the church and you, bundled up in furs, as if you were going to Midnight Mass in broad daylight...

You watched all of that, Eugénie Melanson, and yet...

And yet, you were lovelier than all the dreams pressed flat against the glass on a June day when, here, just as on every other day in June, nothing happened

You were lovelier than all the Vatican Medals given to the dignitaries whose names your husband sometimes mentioned and whose photographs you sometimes saw in the newspaper.

And today...

Today, all of you are here

You are imprisoned, you, the Vatican Medals, the painting of the

Expulsion, the linen flag that Monsignor Richard had made, and all the dreams that lived behind this huge glass of nostalgia. You are at the end of a corridor and you watch the children coming to look at the blue display cases without even noticing your small photo, lost in black and white
But you are the loveliest, Eugénie Melanson, lovelier than Philomène Leblanc, lovelier than Valentine Gallant, lovelier than Euphrémie Blanchard smiling on the arm of Évariste Babineau, lovelier than the Vatican Medals, than Champlain's signature, than the wax seals of the King of England, the King of France, or the King of Spain
You are lovelier because I love you
Because you were unaware of the Gibson Girls, the suffragettes, Barnum's Circus, the Beverley Folies, the Wright Brothers and Thomas Edison, and because you fell asleep near the lace-lined cradles
You should have awakened
You should have awakened because that was the moment that the urge to die gripped your body
You should have awakened, Eugénie Melanson,
But you fell asleep in your body, your body slumbering, thinking about the blue display cases, Champlain's signature, Fort Beaubassin, the cannons of French ships opening fire as they returned to the harbour at Île Saint-Jean.

You fell asleep
You fell asleep while dreaming
You fell asleep while dreaming of new expulsions.

LONG LIVE AMERICA!

Through the mouths of doors wide open
No one will see you again, never again! Never! Never!
No one will see the doors, because there is nothing behind them.
No one will ever see the sun, ever again,
the many suns, their magnificent mouths,
their bright smiles,
like yellow happy faces pasted all over the place.
The tiles are blue, bluer than the sun is yellow.
The corridors are haunted by doors,
doors that yawn in our faces when we pass in front of them or behind
them or beside them or between them,
but somewhere else, Christ, somewhere else!
The sexual adventures of Martin the Great Door
are presented to you today by the United Doors of America

LONG LIVE AMERICA
HEAR YE! AMERICA
HEAR YE!

And flags lingering in the sky
and branches clutching to their trees.
Leaves rolling in the grass like goddamn maniacs,
lights turned off watching us from the tops of their lampposts,
offices planted in the silence that knows
but waited because in offices they know so much about waiting
the nausea because they know so much about waiting.
Trees rolling in the sky, dead bodies wanting for memories in warehouses
of rusty old bones hanging as they do at Swift's, where they throw their
garbage into the Petitcodiac River just because they can.
And the dead animal waste for the profit of Swift Meat!
It accuses us but it means nothing! Nothing! Nothing!

WHEN I BECOME A PATRIOT

To Raymond, to Paul-Eugène,
and to all the Acadian patriots!

To the most lavish farewell
the land could possibly offer
Like the suns in spring
when they are aware of becoming too hot
To dying because everyone must go through it
Between you with your eyes like geese in full flight or like starving seagulls
With the sound of the ocean
With the faded greenish landscapes of the last few days of Acadie wanting
to die

As though the earth were about to open
As though the ocean were about to dry up
As though the sun were about to cool
As though I were about to stretch out my hands to reject you
As though you had forgotten me in leaving
As though I were making my last poor comparison
As though I were preparing for my First Communion
With all the accumulating impossibilities

Much higher than the pyramid could carry us
We are birds with stones in our stomachs
I am the Me of my next wordless love
Out in the storm
The shipwreck of my delusions
The absurd enumeration of all the consequences of my madness
The unrelenting alienation of the storm
The greenish sea that dims in an Acadie before the flood
Before we climb into the ark that has not been built
To die because everyone has to go through it
Before picking up stones in our hands to overcome our weakness
Before dipping our flag in blood and making a lovely mark with it
somewhere
Before the snow falls in all its colours
The thirty seconds before the sky begins to crack
To say that we will have to grow taller because we are too old to climb
trees
To take our heart in our hands and give it a kick
How do we arrive at the music or the words to please them

The last song like the litany of a hangman
An Acadie where there are too few of us and we all seem the same
How shall we write fear, talk fear, say fear, how shall I take the name of
Joe Fear the way others can smile and sign their names on the back of their
cheques and say that their names are Joe Tenderness or Sun or Moon or
Sky, which fall on our backs because we are still praying to the saints in
their heaven
How shall we say that we no longer want to be folksy, that we no longer
want to be the guinea pigs for *L'Acadie, L'Acadie*, that we no longer want
to be the welfare capital of the world, that we no longer want to thirst for
the almighty dollar, that we no longer want to be on standby in a circus or
a television studio or a zoo
How shall we say that we may have nothing to say, that we are sinking
as if we were still on the rotting boats of Colonel Monckton and that we
are leaving for Louisiana, that we are happy because no doubt there were
Acadians who were happy on the rotting boats of Colonel Monckton
The winds of defeat blow over us, the storm is going to defile us.

We are afraid to look at our children who are the extension of our
helplessness, our fear, our defeatism
How shall we help them understand, feel, live the idea that Acadie is not a
leper, that we no longer want the charity of others, that we no longer want
to be told we are sick with leprosy

Questions

Is it possible that one day Acadians will begin to love how well they love?

Answer: Yes   No   Undecided
Other...........................

Is it possible that one day we will be accepted as humans and not as an exceedingly rare species of primate that has barely evolved (Léon Thériault)?

Answer: Yes   No   Undecided
Other...........................

Is it possible that one day we will stop enjoying paternalism and that we will stop believing in it (Paul-Eugène LeBlanc)?

Answer: Yes   No   Undecided
Other...........................

Is it possible that one day we stop selling ourselves and all that we have (Raymond LeBlanc)?

Answer: Yes   No   Undecided
Other...........................

Is it possible that one day we will stop believing that fear will win out over the power to open our hands and grow and die on our feet in an Acadie that is owed to us, that belongs to us and which we must reclaim?

Answer: Yes   No   Undecided
Other.............................

Unless we die in Richibouctou Village from a bullet to the heart.

BLUE

Acadie is no more. There is no longer a black boat in the sea with white sails gliding across the water, our sea, our Atlantic, our desire to slip away to the ends of the earth, but we are already at the end of the earth. There is no longer the blue sailboat where my father spent half his life between the blue of the sky and the blue of the sea. And I would stop writing if I didn't know that the one hope of seeing a new crew is the one already taking form in the eyes of my father who is setting sail in his own Acadie, beyond mine, an Acadie that is no longer a hell but a longing to take down the axes from the barn walls and say that's enough, we've reached the end of the world, we have to bury it or be buried ourselves. And I have begun to wonder if one day this crew will take to the sea with the sun at its back, if one day this crew will take to the sea in front of my mother who prays to blue madonnas for my white sins and does not want to see red blood on the white snow or a black flag in the blue sky, my mother, her nails broken from digging too much in the earth and who may have already learned to say in English "PLEASE."

WHITE

We are at the end of the earth, taxis do not come this far, not into the woods, not into the clouds, taxis will not come to find us on the frozen bay, nor will tanks or jet planes, taxis do not come, nobody comes this far. The snow falls in screens, it is the ends of the earth, the snow falls like a wide sheet on a wide bed for an all-too-beautiful love that is not coming or cannot come this far.

RED

Acadie, my all-too-beautiful, desecrated love, you whom I will never take into the white sheets that you have torn to make white flags like the fields of snow you have sold, like your old fence posts, like your old barns, your old legends, your old dreams, white as an old wedding dress in an old cedar chest. Acadie, my all-too-beautiful, desecrated love, who speaks on credit to say the things that must be paid in cash, who borrows privileges while believing she is obtaining rights. Acadie, my all-too-beautiful, desecrated love, on standby on every continent, on standby in every galaxy, carved up by steeples that are too narrow filled with saints up to the heavens that are too far away. Tear off your blue dress, place red stars on your breasts, plunge into the sea, the red sea that will open up for you as it parted for the flight out of Egypt; the sea belongs to us, it's true, the whole sea belongs to us because we cannot sell it, because no one can buy it.

YELLOW

Acadic melts like a rock in the sun, quietly we melt under the suns of
methane and plastic and steel, the world's strongest collective humiliation
of patience and reason, we understand all, we understand that after having
asked politely we are told we have too much, we know how to say "please
a moment please pardon me please thank you so very much please don't
bother please I don't mind please" and again "you're welcome please come
again please any time please don't mention it please PLEASE PLEASE
PLEASE please kill us please draw the curtain please laugh at us please
treat us like shit please," the first word we learn to say and the last one
that we say to them is "please. Please, make us a beautiful ghetto, not in
a territory, no, no, right in us, make each of us a ghetto, take your time
please." We melt like a rock in the heat of indifference of tolerance of
diplomacy of bilingualism of social assistance of narrow-mindedness of the
patenting of the sun of the ostrichization of our perspective on the world of
the chronic crawling-on-our-knees of standby please standby one two three
TEST TEST TEST.

AND…BLACK

On the television, Pearson's funeral, rolling down avenues black limousines, soft black, dangerous black, armoured black, soldiers marching in black and white. Outside the white snow that darkens, the cameras rolling for glory, cameras marching, their eyes wandering over the white dignitaries, blanked of all suspicion, the white of the rolling clouds and the hidden sun, the white of the white cassocks singing Bach and Handel in the white cathedral, chromed like white steel, and flags flapping in the white breeze against the black sky. Les Anglais marching slowly, safely in their own country, their own cathedrals, their own religion, their own rights along the king's road, their own king on their green dollar bills, English green like grey-green, like London grey. Les Anglais marching in their own light, organs, violins, voices pumping like the colours of numbered regiments, the colours hanging from the ends of the staffs and planted in the walls of steel cathedrals erected to last until death, black death in the black limousines rolling today in black and white, rolling through stormy weather.

HEART OF STEEL

Heart in molten steel like an abandoned city along castles of steel and birds of lead flying over wind-filled cities.

Flowers threatening to close in the fall, coming soon.

Music about to slow down and freeze in the winter in our bodies, elsewhere.

And the silence between two claps of thunder, the last flower of steel that will open perhaps.
The whole earth still blue.
And we began our journey. We came upon a city of gilded buses, the world in colour, steel palaces and white porcelain trains plunging through the night at the speed of lights glowing on the edge of the city near the water. Lights reflected on the water as on winter ice, buses that glimmer like sunstones, with people waving to each other, with children drawing their dreams in colour on the barricades.

The visitors and the princes imprisoned in spaceships, the beautiful stars spinning their points of light around our eyes and the suns that burn on the other side of the planet. On your body between two suns, on my body between two winters, with buses full of dreams that do not stop. Tomorrow morning the sun will glue itself to the roof of the sky.

I left, falling asleep in a train of broken porcelain, travelling through the darkness, towards the end of that day. And I woke up in another country, with my identity cards, with an astonishing credit in a foreign bank. A bank that opens at midnight and closes at eight in the morning, cheque books to buy fields of stars. People asking me the colour of the sky, people asking me if it went well, people asking me the time. And me replying with whatever they want to hear.

TO LIVE AND DIE IN SCOUDOUC

Scoudouc like a vast night lying across the sky
Scoudouc where are you I hear the lament of the loneliest night of your
despair
I have come to see the end like a sky torn into the shape of the end of
the world because I did not know how to wait for the end in the shape
of a red satin heart trimmed with white lace because it seemed to me
that I would see the end if I reached Scoudouc a place all alone and wide
as a gaping hole
Scoudouc was calm flattened in the sun flattened against the earth like
a leaf
Flattened and so calm that I could hear the flies the trees and the grass
that moved the earth as it plunged its roots into the heart of this planet
compacted and hard as a brick

But the green of the grass growing in Scoudouc was a circus that opened plastic doors in my heart to a place where the colours poured in where the sensations of the world rushed across my skin
I got out of the car
I can still hear the click of the door closing and the strange quake that shook the entire car and the door that collapsed into the metal frame and the chrome handle that sparkled in the sun in the time it took for the light to move between the trees and my damp hand
I felt my feet on the hot asphalt and the sound of blood running crazy from one end of my body to the other cascading through my veins like a waterfall
In front of me on the pavement stood Mr. Clean the lascivious slave of soap commercials that gave me joy throughout my childhood sponsored by Proctor and Gamble
And the Man from Glad who looked like Mr. Clean and put the garbage in green plastic bags left for French-Canadian garbagemen
And the Ajax White Knight who fell from his horse waving his lance from side to side
They were all there and they understood nothing

Why had they come to disturb this peaceful day in a Scoudouc where my
love of fun lived on this heap of manure and waved bye-bye to the flies in
love with sugar cubes
Why had they come when Scoudouc was like a lunatic praying locked up
in her little two-steeple church?
Why had they come?
Maybe because Scoudouc was filthy
Maybe because their spacecraft had run out of fuel between two planets
and they had chosen the grass of Scoudouc to make up lost time
The nice soft grass of Scoudouc that tasted like lamb in winter and the sun
in autumn
I dragged my feet in the field
I felt I should be hiding in the high grass of happiness from the tender
despair of eccentricity and the epic sensuality of the 7th century when
the Arabs invented the stirrup and embarked on their conquest of the
Christian world the collapsed American dream perpetrating purple death
like white lilacs hanging from the trees in grape clusters
Scoudouc became cold, cold, cold, it was winter or if it wasn't then it may
as well have been

Scoudouc was lost in a night that did not exist a night too dark or not dark
enough that had settled into the heart of things, that had plunged into
solitude
Scoudouc was lost
The sun tunnelled into the blazing heart of the earth
The sun sank as it might have risen as it might have burst like an egg and
burned Scoudouc with its yolk as if it had been sinking down from the sky
ten nights in a row
I went back to the place where I had left the car
I found a shovel and I dug myself a hole
I lay down in my hole, I pulled a blanket of green grass over my head
And I moved into the night one more time
I was afraid because there was no electric light I cannot sleep without
electric lights without knowing that there is someone who gives me light
I felt the roots of the grass under my back and I realized that I was feeding
the grass
I heard the intimacy of the earth I was trapped in the earth's vagina
I could hear the rocks sliding and the roots plunging and stirring through
the planet
The trees stretching and puncturing the sky
I could not give myself to death

I had to get up I had to live outside to feel the wind from my pores to feel
once again my hand full of dirt against the chrome door of the car stopped
somewhere in my brain
I hear again the "click" and the door opening like a woman's body like a
paradise like the universe
The door swinging wide open and pushing into my face the rancid odour
of hot vinyl
I looked up into the air
The clouds loosened in the hollows of the sky and began to sink in an
unsettling movement towards the kingdom of Scoudouc
Static and suddenly the most beautiful sound in the world
The Gospel coming out of the Cosmos like rock stars with angels in
silver polyethylene robes trumpeting in my throat the sensation of a night
spent outside my body my heart flying on an airplane back from a foreign
country in a lead box hard like melting snow
I turned up the volume on the radio as loud as I could so that my ears
could hear the anthem of my century which might be the last
Scoudouc became a cathedral with arches and angels in the arcades
performing obscene gestures

Scoudouc became a cathedral with the car its Ark of the Covenant the
motor idling and the combustion poisoning the faithful in their robes of
white praying in silence
I came out into the silence of the sky still blue and the trees still reaching
with their roots to collect the relics of the last century
The labels of Chiclet boxes the tin cans the half-rusted tins of Carnation
milk chip bags stamped envelopes letters from the past torn open windows
barred and bolted cigarette butts and pop bottles in the heart of the wild
I placed all of them on the cleanest earth the cleanest grass and I begged
the planet Scoudouc and the entire universe to bless the worshippers of
despair of a heaven too low
Because to speak shouldn't be too much to ask
it's not drinking the ocean it's swallowing the sky
it's as if everyone who speaks
consumes a large quantity of air
it's blue
when photographed from the moon

THE HOUSE OF SILENCE

APRIL 25, 1974 INVENTORY

A — Habitat and Geographical Considerations

The house bundled up in its silence heard the hammering of piano notes
in a minor key running from one end of the corridor to the other repeating
loudly that 3 and 3 make 7 more than ever before.

The house caught between the heat of the night
and the car headlights narrowing
in the daylight, thinking of the absorbing
luminescence of tungsten suns.
The house hid itself in the dark while the high priests sliced the night
with torches to bring forth pieces of field converted into a tabernacle of
technological idols.

The night of robots with eyes of sapphire pushing their metallic audacity
into our dormitories.

The rosaries of the house copulated with the asphalt of the highways and
the suicidal games of pale grass dying to escape slow digestion, ascetic
torture in the viscera of horses with unbridled tentacles.

B — Intermission

In the centre of my enumeration, a palace of glass tubing whines quietly over a mountain of pink cream marshmallow love.

C — Commercial

Let's lie down here and wait for the tide of Dream Whip while the waiter prepares our carafe of kerosene.

D — Flash No. 1

We went outside, absorbed by a cry of bewilderment, at about five o'clock, our hands over our eyes in a gallery of fingers, to see the strident white disks in their agile oscillations like corrosive perforations in the blue silk of a planetarium tremens.

E — Flash no. 2 Post-mortem A: Departure

Then there was a corpse mired in old-fashioned green-and-pink floral satin. Combed and sucking on licorice, he rocked back and forth between two onsets of dizziness. He disappeared but would return later.

F — Flash no. 3 Post-mortem B: Return

A big white crinoline house and once more the stiffness of departures, impatience in the shape of scarcely prepared arrivals or disappearances. The world in metamorphosis in a bottle of Beefeater Gin.

G — Flash no. 4

And the child of paper concepts and pages aligned begins shrieking again at the closing of locked doors. His begging becomes obscene. He runs away and joins a circus after reading a newspaper ad for a juggler who can keep nine rings aloft.

H — Epilogue in a McLuhanesque Illustrative Form

I am near the radio, soon I will be inside the radio, and then I will be the radio. My ears are plugged into the wall, my legs now have four wheels, my eyes travel across the landscape, my fingers escape into outer space and now I am learning to control the knobs that make my lips move.

I — Concrete Application

And when I go into the street the trees stop growing; they hang up their roots and plant themselves, soldiers at attention.

J — Asphyxiating Reflection

I, myself, who have never had a sense of obscurity, me, I'm licking my blood, and I'm incensed that I'm not already robotic.

INVENTORY TWO

The varnished floor
the music filled the room pushing against the walls
the clock ticked it was dark
the ashtray was full of ashes
the paintings seemed as if they were hanging in the void
the cat licked its fur
the books were motionless the doors closed
the objects had become silent
and the pen cast a slanted shadow
the paper was white and the table was blue
the black lamp the flowering cushions
It was the season of cushions
You see, you could never resist a romantic impulse

Les Éditions d'Acadie

MOURIR A SCOUDOUC

HERMÉNÉGILDE CHIASSON

RETURN TO SCOUDOUC

Mourir à Scoudouc was published in 1974, during the fall of the first year I spent in Paris. It was the fourth book published by the now-defunct Éditions d'Acadie. The three others were *Cri de terre* (the first book published in Acadie and also Raymond LeBlanc's first published book), *Comme en Florence* by Léonard Forest, and *Acadie Rock* by Guy Arsenault. We were off to a good start. As I have said elsewhere, it was never my intention to become a writer. The circumstances were simply such that I became one. At the beginning, I had decided to keep a journal—a journal with existential precision, if that makes sense. I started writing the day after student protests were suppressed as a result of the occupation of the science building at the Université de Moncton in which several young leaders of the era had participated. We were all sensing the collapse and chaos of a society accustomed to being silent and which was finally realizing the scope, importance, and power of speaking up publicly and especially to the media. The film *L 'Acadie, l 'Acadie*, which dates from this period, is sometimes screened for later generations who are stunned by the forcefulness of the consciousness-raising that coincided with the founding of the Université de Moncton less than five years earlier, and the sense of hope that this event created.

At the time, I was teaching at Vanier High School in Moncton, and at night I would go to the campus to write articles that would later be published in the student newspaper; Michel Blanchard was the editor at the time. We had developed a biting sense of sarcastic humour, and I can still hear the bursts of laughter that echoed long into the night. It seems that every revolution begins with a huge eruption of laughter, and I have no doubt that it would have been true for us had it not been for those in power who decided to act tough and barred most of the student leaders from campus.

One afternoon in June, I was walking around in the Musée acadien, and I was struck with the idea, as was often the case, that the only legacy we could offer were some old objects, a testimony to a timid and impoverished culture. We had dreamed of modernity and the dream had suddenly come to an end. I decided at that moment that I should write about this period accurately, so that later I could reread my journal and recall my state of mind. When I returned home, I wrote "Eugénie Melanson," a piece that, at first, I intended to keep to myself. But a series of events and circumstances conspired to make it a reference point, a liminal text for my first book, although, at the time, the idea of publishing a book was far from my mind.

Time passed. From the end of the 1960s to the early years of the 1970s, I had other responsibilities and other endeavours. I was focussed on my work as a visual artist, on my studies at Mount Allison University, and later my job at Radio-Canada. The French broadcasting network was growing and expanding its Acadian programming. For the first time, a voice was being given to culture as well as the news, which until then had been Radio-Canada's only mission. At the same time, I was engaged in all kinds of projects, including the publication of *L'Anti-Livre* with Jacques and Gilles Savoie, a venture that predated the founding of Éditions d'Acadie by just a few months. I was part of a group of artists that included Francis Coutellier, Pavel Skalnik, Georges Goguen, Edward Léger, and André Thériault, whose

work was being exhibited all over the province and even abroad. I was still writing but had no interest in publishing. My only interest was modernity, which, to my mind, meant nothing more than a desire to join the rest of the world and to take part in a relevant, contemporary venture. Where did this desire come from? No doubt from a curiosity that has never left me, a curiosity that privileges research over repetition and conscience over success. It allowed me to avoid the trap of careerist ambition so I could always push myself towards whatever would further my fascination with discourse and the way it enabled sharing and communication.

Before *Cri de terre* was published, Raymond LeBlanc had asked me to design the cover of the book and the ink drawings found in the interior. Since he knew I was writing, he did me a favour by including me in the program for the poetry reading he was planning for the launch. I had never before seen so many people at such an event, nor have I ever since. Nor had I witnessed such enthusiasm, itself a testimony to the life force of a literature

CHER HERMÉNÉGILDE,

— SOUS L'ÉGIDE D'HERMÈS,
J'APPRENDS QUE TU
VIENS D'INVENTER LA
MACHINE À RENOUVELER
L'ESPACE QUOTIDIEN
NE MENT,
QUE TEL EST TON
PROJET D'EXPOSITION.
— QUE VOILA UNE GRANDE
POÉTIQUE DE PEINTRE!
QUOI CON EN DISE.

J'Y SERAI,
MERDE!

Le homard musical
rides again

CANADA

HERMAN CHIASSON
PEINTRE
GALERIE D'ART
UNE HIVER CITÉ
MONT QUETONNE
NOTA BENE

1972

just then being born. I had planned to read the poems about the colours of the flag ("Blue," "White," "Red," "Yellow," and "And…Black") and "Eugénie Melanson." I began by reading "Eugénie Melanson," but I didn't even make it to the second poem. I was overcome by an emotion I did not understand and could only describe much later. There is, between the act of writing and the act of publishing, a transition that gives writing a social dimension and a presence made larger by the fact that it is starting to circulate and be shared. The words become a carrier of a consciousness—something which will be part of the writer's work for the rest of their life—and possibly even beyond. This phenomenon was new to Acadie. It certainly was new to me and to Raymond who, that evening, marked his entry into literature.

Once I had finished reading, still feeling rather shaken, I walked downstairs from la Cube, the café/bar in the Arts building, where the launch was being held, and came face-to-face with Melvin Gallant, the founder and first editor of Les Éditions d'Acadie, and Pierre-André Arcand, who was then the poetry editor. The two of them asked me if I had other poems like the one I had just read. Then they told me they were determined to publish them. Not long after, Pierre-André Arcand and Pierre L'Hérault convinced me to spend some time going over my poetry with them, choosing the poems for a book and determining what had to be done to make them publishable. I could see absolutely no reason for this interest, because for me the books I wanted to write would represent radical positions in favour of modernity, something I could see absolutely no trace of in my poems, which, I felt, were written in more of a romantic tradition. As far as I was concerned, this was a journal and publishing it would carry the same risk as publishing personal letters or other pieces people are better off keeping to themselves. A poem like "Eugénie Melanson," for example, seemed to me to be much too complacent and much too conventional. As always, I felt that modernity should exhibit a militant drive towards confrontation. Yes, people would be shocked at first, but then they would rally together and, by so doing, bestow a certain amount of fame upon the author—the dream of every artist.

Vendredi, 9 février, 1968

The title of the book that would later be published was inspired by *Mourir à Madrid*, Frédéric de Rossif's beautiful film about the Spanish Civil War, in which I had heard the poetry of Federico García Lorca.[1] I replaced Madrid with Scoudouc, a place announced on a large directional sign on the highway, although at the time it was virtually impossible to figure out where this mythical place might be, even when driving in that direction. It made me think of Acadie, a place with no geographical beginning or end. As for "to die," it seemed to me that people died in Acadie more often than they lived. The idea really was not very optimistic and several people, including Gérald Leblanc, often reproached me for my pessimism or for what, at the very least, appeared to be pessimism, although I had considered myself to be more of a realist. The form that I chose was prose poetry, an approach to the poetic form that I have almost always followed thereafter.

---

1 Translator's note: The English version of this film is entitled *To Die in Madrid*; we chose *To Live and Die in Scoudouc* as a reference to both Rossif's film and the popular thriller *To Live and Die in LA*.

I find poetry can be found anywhere, not simply in a single configuration of lines and verses that, in any event, are often chopped-up prose anyway. The book was divided into five sections: the first, "To," is a dedication of sorts; then poems about love, life, and nostalgia in "Between the Season..."; followed by poems inspired by politics in "Acadie, My All-Too-Beautiful Love"; the long narrative poem "To Live and Die in Scoudouc"; and the formalist poems of "The House of Silence." I did the page layout for the book myself and also took the photographs, although in conditions much more difficult than those under which we produced the new French edition, for which I also did the design and page layout. For the new edition, I had much more direct control over the final result, which no doubt explains why, in the original version, there are two completely blank pages. Things were not planned that way, but in the end, they were accepted perhaps to indulge the author's whims.

During the summer of 1974, once my work was done, I left for a road trip across Canada and down the west coast of the US to Los Angeles. I returned via Las Vegas and Chicago. While I was away, Pierre-André Arcand forwarded some poems to *Les Écrits du Canada français*. Their publication attracted a lot of attention, especially in an article in *Le Devoir* where the reviewer, Jean-Éthier Blais, interpreted them as an indication of the vitality of Acadian francophones and, by extension it seems, of francophones throughout Canada. He was particularly effusive about my work. The same thing happened in *Le Jour*, where Gaëtan Dostie ended his article by writing that he hoped I would soon publish a book. When I returned from my trip, I met with Pierre-André, who told me about the articles. At first I thought it was a hoax, like some of the other pranks he had pulled, but when I read them myself I had to accept them as proof that my life had just changed and that it was time to start getting used to the idea of being a writer. I have to admit that this realization made me uncomfortable. I was born into family in which my father and mother were illiterate. I grew up in a house and a community in which there were almost no books. Such a realization could

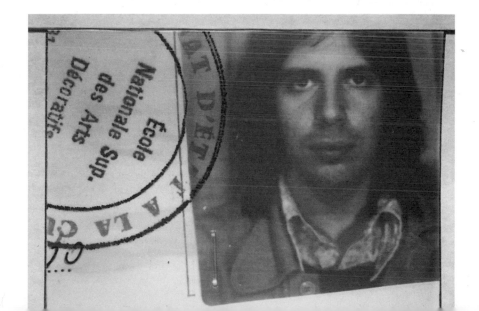

not help but make my head spin. It seemed that it would take me a whole lifetime to recover from the intoxicating dizziness. In the fall, I left for Paris to begin working on a master's degree and a PhD, starting in visual arts at École nationale supérieure des arts décoratifs and later in aesthetics at Université de Paris I (the Sorbonne). *Mourir à Scoudouc* was published in the fall, shortly after I left for Paris. Pierre-André had decided to print an initial run of two thousand copies, something that would be unthinkable today. I was not at the launch, but I learned about it through the mail. Marie-Reine Martin, the producer I had worked with at Radio-Canada, sent me a tape, a copy of a story that had been broadcast nationally and discussed the "great quality of my writing." Other reviews, all just as positive, added to the strange impression that I was living a double life which, unbeknownst even to me, was already becoming divided between words and images.

Deep down, I was happy I did not have to face the public at the launch, especially at that point in my life, because public appearances were always difficult for me. This may be why I chose these two vocations — visual arts and writing — both are rather private occupations that allow me to be seen without my having to be present or perform as would a musician or an actor. I also have to add that this type of event has now become common in Acadie, but at the time, the enthusiasm was a demonstration of the excitement with which Acadians greeted any new cultural activity, particularly public arts events.

When I returned to Moncton in the summer of 1975, Gaëtan Dostie had organized an event called le Solstice de la poèsie Québécoise, five long readings that were part of the cultural program which ran in parallel to the Montréal Olympics. Paul Savoie, Calixte Duguay, and I were the only three poets from outside Québec invited to this event. It was at this reading that I met Renaud Longchamp, Michel Beaulieu, Pierre Morency, and Gaston Miron, whom I would see many times thereafter and who told me that he

had loved "Eugénie Melanson." I would learn later that Miron's mother was also named Eugénie.

Again in 1975, this time in May, the journal of the Université de Moncton published an issue with a "si que" feature section on my writing. The first "si que" feature had been dedicated to Antonine Maillet. There was something bold and pretentious about venturing into this novel territory. I had only published one book and who knew if there would be others. Pierre-André Arcand, who was editing the section, asked me for unpublished work. He also included a long interview with me and an article written by Alain Masson that ended with the following words: "If he were a French poet, he would be Hugo; if he were a Québéc poet, Miron; an American, William Carlos Williams; an Italian, Eugenio Montale; a Chilean, Pablo Neruda. But in any event, he is an Acadian poet." It was yet another thing to make my head spin.

In December of the same year, Yolande Lefèbvre, the librarian at the Canadian Cultural Centre in Paris, told me that she was organizing a launch of *Mourir à Scoudouc* in Paris. She had also invited Melvin Gallant and Marielle Boudreau, another author who had published with Éditions d'Acadie. The program would end with a screening of Léonard Forest's film, *Les Acadiens de la dispersion*. There would also be speeches, and Melvin would first offer a long presentation on Acadian society, emphasizing the cultural vitality that was emerging on this side of the Atlantic.

Mourir à Scoudouc was a popular success, particularly if one compares its sales with those of poetry collections published today, including my own collections. In an interview on France Culture, the interviewer simply could not get over the fact that we had sold four thousand copies of the book. For him, even in France, this was something of a phenomenon. Shortly thereafter, Les Éditions de l'Hexagone, which Gaston Miron managed at the time, proposed to co-publish an edition of *Mourir à Scoudouc* with Éditions d'Acadie, although he proposed using a different paper, since the original paper would have been far too expensive. It is true that the quality of the original edition would have been difficult to replicate. We had, no doubt, proceeded without much thought and without realizing how costly the venture would be. After Éditions d'Acadie closed in 2000, *Mourir à Scoudouc* went out of print. It was reissued by Éditions de l'Interligne and reprinted twice as part of the Bibliothèque Canadienne-française collection. But now, I am especially happy that Serge Patrice Thibodeau and Les Éditions Perce-Neige have produced a new edition, which marks the return of the book to Acadie and once again with attention to book design.

In 1977, the house in which I stored my archives burned to the ground. Everything was destroyed in the fire... This "memory" edition suffers from that loss. The availability of the original documents and images would have made this edition a more faithful representation of the original and one of greater historical significance. Instead, this book is a re-creation that tries to replicate the original but with the distance and the distortion that time invariably brings to this kind of enterprise.

It goes without saying that revisiting this book and the period in which it was written represents, for me, a nostalgic experience that is somewhat overwhelming. The book starts with death and continues into an adventure which, from book to book, would become lighter and lighter, more effervescent and perhaps even fantastical. The period lent itself to a particular process in which political aspirations aligned with the writing in the first books published in the 1970s. Professor and critic Raoul Boudreau describes these books as the founding texts of Acadian poetry. It was only much later that the discourse would shift towards the more personal and the more quotidian, a shift that results in less attachment among readers who are less personally engaged than they were by the angry poems that spoke directly to them and called them to action. Aspects of that political engagement may be found in *Mourir à Scoudouc*, but there is also much more. The poet Yolande Villemaire once told me that in your first book, you want to say everything, in the sense that you are already tracing out your life's work. When I look at this book, I can, indeed, see the overarching themes that reoccur in my work. I have the impression that, whatever we might do to try to escape, we always end up writing the same book over and over again, hoping to make it better, hoping eventually to place a period at the end of a sentence that seems to have no end. It's a little like the idea with which Roland Barthes ends his *Critical Essays*. Writes Barthes, "One writes in order to be loved, one is read without being able to be loved."[2] And so, with each new book, we are forced to try yet again.

---

2 Roland Barthes, *Critical Essays*, translated from the French by Richard Howard. Evanston: Northwestern University Press, 1972.

Je suis né une journée d'hiver en 46 à 5 hres du matin à St Simon village de 960 habitants accrolé à la cité Nord du N.B. Fils de pêcheur cadet. Ensuite je me suis quelque peu préoccupé d'atteindre à St Simon remarquable, Moncton et Sackville à qui m'a valu le droit et le privilège d'exercer l'activité d'artiste peintre et les noms moins officielles, ..., d'enseignant, de caricaturiste, d'illustrateur, de recherche graphiste, d'annoviste, de journaliste, de chargé d'enseignement et j'en passe et pas toujours les meilleures. "Somewhere along the road" j'ai rencontré M. Blanchard, R. Leblanc, A. Maillet, ... Fanest ... Roussel, R. Savoie, G. Leblanc, P. A. Arsend, ... Lacroix, C. Molina ... Buers, J. Ricordeau qui m'a dit que je faisais partie d'une catégorie de gens qui après avoir pris 2 verres, sont prêts à fraterniser avec toute l'humanité, lui, Ricordeau, n'étant évidemment pas de ... catégorie, Passons. J'ai commencé à écrire sur l'acad en 61 et depuis cette "réalité" est devenu le centre de mes préoccupations littéraires. Je ne crois pas qu'il s'agisse d'un choix conscient mais plutôt d'une circonstance inévitable de la prise de la parole. Je suis mort à ... coudeur en 72. C'est à dire que je suis mort à une certaine acade Reste maintenant à en trouver une autre

ABOUT THE AUTHOR

Herménégilde Chiasson is an iconic figure in Acadian art, society, and culture. His prolific body of work in literature, visual arts, film, and theatre includes over thirty plays and fifty books. He is the recipient of numerous awards, including the Governor General's Literary Award for Poetry, an Award of Excellence for film and the Pascal-Poirier Award of Excellence for literature from the Government of New Brunswick, the Molson Prize, the Prix France-Acadie and Prix Éloizes, the Grand Prix International de poésie de Langue Française Léopold Sédar Senghor, the Prix quinquennal Antonine-Maillet-Acadie Vie, the Grand Prix de la francophonie canadienne, and many others. He is a Chevalier de l'Ordre français des Arts et des Lettres, and a member of the Ordre des francophones d'Amérique, the Royal Canadian Academy of Arts, the Order of Canada and the Order of New Brunswick. He is also the recipient of numerous honorary doctorates. Chiasson holds an MA in Fine Arts from the State University of New York and a PhD from the Sorbonne. He served as New Brunswick's Lieutenant Governor from 2003 to 2009. He now lives in Grand-Barachois with Marcia Babineau, a leading figure in French-language theatre, where he continues to write, paint, photograph, and produce works of the imagination and to advocate for the arts in New Brunswick, Canada, and throughout the world.

ABOUT THE TRANSLATOR

Jo-Anne Elder has translated many of Chiasson's works of poetry, including *Beatitudes* and *Conversations* and, in collaboration with Fred Cogswell, *Climates*. She and Fred Cogswell also translated and edited *Unfinished Dreams*, the first anthology of Acadian poetry published in English.

L'Anti-Livre (with Jacques Savoie and Gilles Savoie), photos, poems, drawings, Éditions de l'Étoile Maganée, 1972; *Mourir à Scoudouc*, poetry, Éditions d'Acadie, 1974; *Rapport sur l'État de mes illusions*, poetry, Éditions d'Acadie, 1976; *Mourir à Scoudouc*, poetry, 2nd edition, Éditions d'Acadie/Les Éditions de l'Hexagone, 1979; *Les Acadiens* (with Barry Ancelet and Antonine Maillet), non-fiction, Éditions DMR, 1984; *Claude Roussel* (with Patrick Laurette), non-fiction (art), Éditions d'Acadie, 1985; *Atarelle et les Pakmaniens*, children's theatre, Éditions Michel Henry, 1986; *Prophéties*, poetry, Éditions Michel Henry, 1986; *Vous*, poetry, Éditions d'Acadie, 1991; *l'Événement Rimbaud* (with Claude Beausoleil and Gérald Leblanc), poetry, Éditions Perce-Neige/Écrits des Forges, 1991; *Existences*, poetry, Éditions Perce-Neige/ Écrits des Forges, 1991; *Vermeer*, poems and photos, Éditions Perce-Neige/Écrits des Forges, 1992; *Miniatures*, poetry, Éditions Perce-Neige, 1995; *Aliénor*, theatre, Éditions d'Acadie, 1998; *Climats*, poetry, Éditions d'Acadie, 1996; *Conversations*, poetry, Éditions d'Acadie, 1998; *Climates* (translated by Jo-Anne Elder and Fred Cogswell), poetry, Goose Lane Editions, 1999; *Pour une culture de l'injure* (with Pierre Raphaël Pelletier), non-fiction, Éditions du Nordir; *Brunante*, prose, Éditions XYZ, 2000; *Actions*, poetry, Éditions Trait d'union, 2000; *Légendes*, prose, Éditions J'ai VU, 2000; *Laurie ou la vie de galerie*, theatre, La Grande Marée/Prise de parole, 2001; *Conversations* (translated by Jo-Anne Elder and Fred Cogswell), poetry, Goose Lane Editions, 2002; *Available Light* (translated by Wayne Grady), prose, Douglas and McIntyre, 2002; *L'oiseau tatoué*, poetry, La courte échelle; *Répertoire*, poetry, Écrits des Forges/Le dé bleu, 2003; *Émergences*, poetry, Les Éditions L'Interligne, 2003; *Parcours*, poetry, Éditions Perce-Neige, 2005; *Le Christ est apparu au Gun Club*, theatre, Prise de parole, 2005; *Lifedream* (translated by Jo-Anne Elder), theatre, Guernica, 2006; *Béatitudes*, poetry, Prise de parole, 2007; *Beatitudes* (translated by Jo-Anne Elder), poetry, Goose Lane Editions, 2007; *Solstices*, poetry, Éditions Prise de parole, 2009; *Le cœur de la tempête* (with Louis-Dominique Lavigne), theatre, Éditions Prise de parole, 2010; *Pierre Hélène et Michel / Cap Enragé*, theatre, Éditions Prise de parole, 2012; *Autoportrait*, boxed set of 12 books, poetry, Éditions Prise de parole, 2014, *Voyages et rêves*, limited edition artist's book, poetry, Frog Hollow Press, 2018; *Trajets, trajectoires, traversées*, poetry, Les Éditions de La Grenouillère, 2018.